BABY ANIMALS

MY FIRST DOT TO DOT

Activity Book

This book belongs to

be Aitana

turtle

camel

hippo

iguana

chick

1
2
3
4
5
6
7

porcupine

meerkat

1
2
3
4
5
6
7
8

elephant

chipmunk

tiger

A B C D E F G H

frog

sea turtle

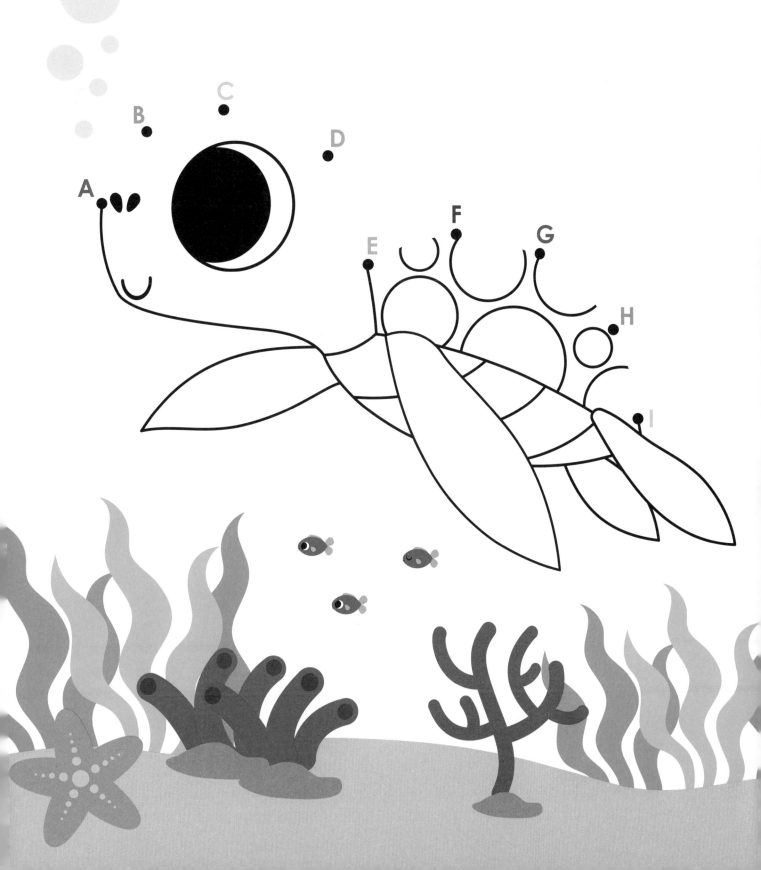

penguin

bear

emu

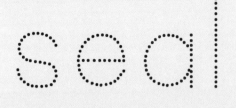

seal

A
B
C
D
E
F
G
H
I

cheetah

horse

lemur

pig

panda

lion

giraffe

bunny

10
1
9
2
8
3
7
4
6
5

A
B
C
D
E
F G H I J

rhino

kangaroo

hedgehog

llama

deer

beaver

zebra

fox

armadillo

squirrel

crocodile

puppy

guinea pig

raccoon

duck

unicorn

lamb

sea lion

shark

mouse

dinosaur

dolphin

hamster

kitten

red panda

Illustrated by Hazel Quintanilla
Designed by Ryan Dunn

Published by Sourcebooks Wonderland,
an imprint of Sourcebooks Kids
P.O. Box 4410, Naperville, Illinois 60567-4410
(630) 961-3900
sourcebookskids.com

Date of Production: March 2022
Run Number: 5025356
Printed and bound in China (LPG)
10 9 8 7 6 5 4 3 2 1

FSC
www.fsc.org

MIX
Paper from
responsible sources
FSC® C020056